My Nose

Brian Enslow

Bailey Books
an imprint of
Enslow Publishers, Inc.
40 Industrial Road
Box 398
Berkeley Heights, NJ 07922
USA

http://www.enslow.com

Bailey Books, an imprint of Enslow Publishers, Inc.

Copyright © 2011 by Enslow Publishers, Inc.

Library of Congress Cataloging-in-Publication Data

Enslow, Brian.

My nose / Brian Enslow.
  p. cm. — (All about my body)
  Summary: "Simple text and photographs present a story about noses"—Provided by
publisher.
  Includes bibliographical references and index.
  ISBN 978-0-7660-3814-1 (alk. paper)
  1. Nose—Juvenile literature. 2. Smell—Juvenile literature. I. Title.
  QP458.E57 2011
  612.2—dc22
                            2010014873

Paperback ISBN: 978-159845-170-2

Printed in the United States of America

052010 Lake Book Manufacturing, Inc., Melrose Park, IL

10 9 8 7 6 5 4 3 2 1

To Our Readers: We have done our best to make sure all Internet Addresses in this book
were active and appropriate when we went to press. However, the author and the publisher
have no control over and assume no liability for the material available on those Internet sites
or on other Web sites they may link to. Any comments or suggestions can be sent by e-mail
to comments@enslow.com or to the address on the back cover.

✪ Enslow Publishers, Inc., is committed to printing our books on recycled paper. The paper
in every book contains 10% to 30% post-consumer waste (PCW). The cover board on the
outside of each book contains 100% PCW. Our goal is to do our part to help young people
and the environment too!

Photo Credits: Shutterstock.com

Cover Photo: Shutterstock.com

Note to Parents and Teachers

Help pre-readers get a jumpstart on reading. These lively stories introduce simple concepts
with repetition of words and short simple sentences. Photos and illustrations fill the pages
with color and effectively enhance the text. Free Educator Guides are available for this series
at www.enslow.com. Search for the *All About My Body* series name.

Contents

Words to Know 3

Story 4

Read More....................... 24

Web Sites 24

Index 24

Words to Know

fish

round

Big nose.

Is this your
nose?

5

Little nose.
Is this your nose?

Long nose.
Is this your nose?

Fish nose.
Is this your nose?

Flat nose.
Is this your nose?

Green nose.
Is this your nose?

**Brown nose.
Is this your nose?**

Round nose.
Is this your nose?

**Nice nose.
Is this your nose?**

Your nose?

My nose.

Read More

Birkett, Georgie. *Is This My Nose?* Hauppauge, N.Y.: Barron's Educational Series, 2008.

Klingel, Cynthia Fitterer. *Nose/La Nariz.* Strongsville, Ohio.: Gareth Stevens Publishing, 2010.

Web Sites

Enchanted Learning.
<http://www.enchantedlearning.com/dictionarysubjects/body.shtml>

Sid Says on PBS Kids.
<http://pbskids.org/sid/#/sidSays>

Index

big, 4

brown, 17

fish, 11

green, 15

little, 7

long, 9, 17, 19, 21, 22, 23

nice, 21

nose, 4, 5, 9, 11,13, 15

round, 19

Guided Reading Level: **B**
Guided Reading Leveling System is based on the guidelines recommended by Fountas and Pinnell.

Word Count: 54